Strange Animals Of The World
First Grade
Science Series

Earth is home to
about 1 million known
animal species.

Aye-aye is one of the strangest looking primates. Aye-aye eats insect larva, nectar, seed, fruit and fungi.

Gerenuk is a long-necked species of antelope. A gerenuk can go its entire life without drinking water.

Babirusa is a member of the pig family. The upper pair of tusks on the male babirusa will grow up through its snout.

Lowland
streaked tenrec
is a small
tenrec found
in Madagascar.
It remains
with its family,
numbering up to
20 individuals in
each burrow.

Saiga antelope is recognizable by an extremely unusual, over-sized, flexible nose structure, the proboscis.

Axolotl is not
a fish, but
an amphibian.
Axolotls can
grow back
body parts
that are lost or
bitten off by
a predator or
another axolotl.

Leafy seadragon is found along the southern and western coasts of Australia. These species can also be called as leafies.